20th Century
PERSPECTIVES

The Causes of World War II

Paul Dowswell

Heinemann
LIBRARY

www.heinemann.co.uk
Visit our website to find out more information about Heinemann Library books.

To order:
 Phone 44 (0) 1865 888066
 Send a fax to 44 (0) 1865 314091
🖥 Visit the Heinemann Bookshop at www.heinemann.co.uk to browse our catalogue and order online.

First published in Great Britain by Heinemann Library,
Halley Court, Jordan Hill, Oxford OX2 8EJ,
a division of Reed Educational and Professional Publishing Ltd.
Heinemann is a registered trademark of Reed Educational and Professional Publishing Ltd.

OXFORD MELBOURNE AUCKLAND
JOHANNESBURG BLANTYRE GABORONE
IBADAN PORTSMOUTH (NH) USA CHICAGO

Produced for Heinemann Library by Discovery Books Ltd
Designed by Ian Winton
Consultant: Stewart Ross
Picture research by Rachel Tisdale
Originated by Dot Gradations
Printed by Wing King Tong in Hong Kong, China

ISBN 0 431 12007 2
06 05 04 03 02
10 9 8 7 6 5 4 3 2 1

British Library Cataloguing in Publication Data
Dowswell, Paul, 1957 –
  The causes of World War II. – (20th century perspectives)
  1.World War, 1939–1945 – Causes – Juvenile literature
  I.Title
  940.5'311

Acknowledgements
Corbis pp. 11, 18, 27, 32; Mary Evans Picture Library pp. 8, 15, 17, 20, 23; Hulton Archive pp. 22, 25, 26, 30, 34, 37, 40; Hulton Deutsch pp. 4, 12, 33, 42; Hulton Getty pp. 6, 13, 16, 21, 28, 29, 35; David King Collection pp. 24, 36; Peter Newark pp. 5, 7; Peter Newark's American Pictures pp. 10, 14; Peter Newark's Military Pictures pp. 19, 38, 43.

Cover photograph of Adolf Hitler being welcomed by German-speaking children in Sudetenland in 1938, reproduced with permission of Hulton Archive.

Any words appearing in the text in bold, **like this**, are explained in the glossary.

Contents

World War Two begins

For the dozen or so German prisoners held by **Nazi SS** soldiers near to the Polish border, the last day of August 1939, was to be the last day of their lives. All had been condemned to death and had passed their final weeks in brutal confinement. Now, herded out of a prison van and into an army barracks, they were ordered to take off their prison clothes and put on the uniform of the Polish army. Outside the window, in the late afternoon light, the sky was cloudless blue, and the sun had baked the earth hard. It was too beautiful a day to be in such strange and terrifying circumstances. Then, one by one, they were led away. What thoughts passed through their minds in their last bewildered moments we will never know, but their fate was to be truly bizarre.

Each man was given an injection which made him unconscious. Then all were carried into another van which was driven to a radio station near to the Polish border. The men were dumped here and there outside the station, and bullets were fired into their bodies. Presently, newspaper journalists and press photographers arrived, to record the whole grisly scene.

War begins

At dawn the next day, 1 September, a German invasion force of some 2 million men poured into Poland. Hitler, the Nazi leader, justified the invasion to the world by claiming it was provoked by a Polish attack on a German radio station. As German bombers destroyed airfields and fuel dumps behind the front line, and attacked the Polish capital of Warsaw, dive bombers, tanks and artillery destroyed Polish front-line troops. This was the world's introduction to *blitzkrieg* – a new form of warfare where **motorized troops** swept rapidly forward following tanks and aircraft. The Polish army fought bravely, but were completely outmatched – they even sent cavalry (soldiers on horses) into action against German tanks. To make matters worse the Soviet Union attacked Poland on the 17 September.

Nazi soldiers march through Poland and into battle in September 1939. World War Two had just begun. The conflict was to continue for nearly six years.

As the German army pushed relentlessly east, Poland's startled peasants could only watch in numb amazement. The arrogant young soldiers in the grey-green uniforms who swept through their towns were frightening enough. But the ones that followed, in their sinister black uniforms and wearing a death's head insignia (a badge or emblem), seemed to have been sent by the devil himself. These men were members of Heinrich Himmler's SS *Einsatzgruppen* (special forces). Their task was to kill anyone thought capable of organizing resistance to the Nazis, like army officers, teachers or academics. In the years that were to follow they were also instructed to round up any Jews they could find. Many were killed where they were found, but others were taken to **ghettos** in Warsaw and other cities and were eventually killed in **concentration camps**. Over the next five and a half years of war, Poland would suffer so badly almost one in five of its population would be killed.

It took barely a month for Poland to be conquered. Hitler and Nazi Germany were now left in possession of the whole of central Europe. The Nazi leader had hoped to gain Poland without stirring up a general European war, but he had miscalculated badly. Within two days of the invasion, France and Britain had both declared war on Germany – so marking the beginning of World War Two.

The Nazis wasted no time in victimizing their enemies. These Polish Jews are being put to work in a forced labour camp near Warsaw, less than a month after the German invasion.

Hitler and Poland

'Close your hearts to pity. Act brutally. Whatever we find in the shape of an upper class in Poland is to be **liquidated** ... [We must] ensure that the Polish **intelligentsia** cannot throw up a new leader class.'

Hitler's orders on the eve of the invasion of Poland, August 1939.

What were the causes of World War Two?

'World War Two' is a term used to describe a succession of wars that took place in different parts of the world between 1939 and 1945. Some historians think the war began in 1937 when Japan invaded China, others give 1939 as the year, when Germany invaded Poland. But these different conflicts only developed into a truly world war when the USA joined the conflict in 1941. The war in Europe ended in May 1945 and in the Far East three months later.

There are many reasons why World War Two started. In this book we will explain some of the most important ones. To begin with we need to look at the effects of the Treaty of Versailles, signed after World War One, and the role of the League of Nations, also established after that war. We will consider the effects of the Great **Depression**, especially in helping to bring to power extreme political regimes such as the **Nazis**. The attitudes and policies of the **Allied** countries described by the terms **'appeasement'** and **'isolationism'** will also be examined. But first we need to look at events that took place earlier in the century when World War One was being fought.

*Flag-waving Londoners, some civilians, some in military uniform, celebrate the **armistice** on 11 November 1918. Little did they realize that the peace was only temporary.*

World War One

World War One (1914–18) was such a terrible, destructive war that those who fought it tried to convince themselves that all the suffering and sacrifice they endured had been for some greater good. During the conflict it was often referred to as the 'Great War'. In fact the Great War merely spawned another, which was much worse. Barely five years after the war ended in 1918, it was already being referred to as 'The *First* World War'.

The causes of World War One were many and complex. Rival **alliances** had been made by opposing European nations, who were building up their armed forces in an effort to gain or maintain military superiority. There was fierce competition over **colonies**. Germany was a powerful, wealthy nation, but she had only a few colonies. Her rivals in Europe,

France and Britain, had huge colonial **empires** mostly in Asia and Africa. These colonies provided **raw materials** and cheap labour, as well as the prestige of being a 'world power'.

Germany, Austria-Hungary and their allies fought Britain, France and their allies in World War One mainly to defend or improve their position in the world. For four years the war in western Europe had been a bloody **stalemate**. But in eastern Europe, Germany had had great success. In early 1918 Germany made peace with its other major enemy, Russia, and gained territory in eastern Europe. With Russia out of the war, Germany turned her full attention to western Europe. But in the summer of 1918, she ran out of steam just when fresh American troops were joining the exhausted Allied armies of Britain and France.

A muddled ending

By November 1918, the German army was in headlong retreat back to its own western borders. Fearing a **communist revolution** in their war-weary nation, similar to the one that had overwhelmed Russia in 1917, Germany's leaders called for peace. But this retreat had been kept from the German people, some of whom still believed their armies were winning the war.

The fighting stopped and complex negotiations began at the Palace of Versailles in France. As a defeated nation Germany had no say in the discussions that took place or in the final terms of the treaty. The **delegates** at the conference decided, rather unfairly, that Germany was responsible for starting the war. German soldiers, and much of German society, were left with a sense of deep betrayal and bitterness at the end of a war that at one time they had appeared to be winning. Nothing they fought for had been achieved, and in the years after the war Germany was to be punished and humiliated.

German war graves on the Western Front in November 1918. These graves represent a tiny fraction of the 10 million soldiers who were killed in World War One.

The Treaty of Versailles

Leaders of the victorious nations of World War One are shown here arriving at the peace talks at Versailles. US President Woodrow Wilson (centre left) strides alongside the French Prime Minister Georges Clemenceau (centre).

'We have won the war; now we have to win the peace, and it may be more difficult.' So spoke French Prime Minister Clemenceau, at the start of the peace conference that was held in the Palace of Versailles in the summer of 1919. Although Germany had called for an **armistice** the previous autumn, it was on the understanding that their country would be treated fairly. But over the winter and spring the attitudes of some of the victors hardened. This was to be a 'make Germany pay' peace, and it resulted in a settlement that no one was happy with.

Making a lasting peace?

The main problem was that the victors were divided on how best to ensure the peace of Europe. US president Woodrow Wilson put forward a set of idealistic proposals concerning free trade and disarmament and the right of nations to decide their own futures. He also proposed the setting up of an international organization for solving quarrels between nations. This organization became known as the League of Nations. These and other ideas were known as the 'Fourteen Points'. Wilson was anxious that there should be **reconciliation** with Germany. Britain and France, represented by their prime ministers David Lloyd-George and Georges Clemenceau had other ideas. Clemenceau was determined that Germany should never again be strong enough to threaten France's position in the world, and so wanted a peace treaty that would leave Germany permanently weak. Lloyd-George wanted a more conciliatory peace, but felt bound to support his wartime **ally** Clemenceau. The fierce hostility that was felt towards Germany by many British politicians and by much of the British public also hampered his position at the conference.

Verdicts on Versailles

'Those who sign this treaty will sign the death sentence of many millions of German men, women and children.'

Count Ulrich von Brockdorff-Rantzau – head of the German delegation.

'We shall have to do the whole thing over again in twenty five years at three times the cost.'

David Lloyd-George – British prime minister.

However, the idea of the League of Nations was accepted and its headquarters were established in Geneva, Switzerland, in 1920. Agreement regarding the fate of Germany was also reached. The main points of the Treaty of Versailles were:

- Germany was to accept responsibility for starting the war.

- She was to pay 'reparations' (compensation) to her former enemies totalling £6,500,000,000.

- Germany lost territory to France, Poland and Belgium. The result of this was that several million Germans now found themselves living in different countries.

- Germany's overseas **colonies** were given to other countries especially Britain, France and Japan.

- The German army was to be restricted to 100,000 men.

- No tanks, aircraft, submarines or heavy artillery were permitted in Germany.

The treaty was signed in June 1919, but it was undermined from the very beginning. Against the wishes of Woodrow Wilson, the American Senate refused to accept the peace treaty. Also they would not allow the USA to join the League of Nations, which they saw as an organization for protecting the position of Britain and France. Wilson, who had already suffered a severe stroke, felt humiliated. With his spirit broken, his health never recovered.

Europe after World War One. As a result of the post war treaties thousands of Germans found themselves living outside the newly created borders of Germany.

Other treaties that changed national boundaries

Alongside Germany three other empires fell during the war — Austria-Hungary, Russia and Ottoman Turkey. Treaties were signed which changed Europe's borders and created new countries. Under the Treaty of Brest-Litovsk (March 1918) Russia lost territory to Finland, Latvia, Estonia, Lithuania and Poland. By the Treaty of St Germain-en Laye (September 1919) Austria lost territory to Czechoslovakia, Yugoslavia, Poland, Hungary and Italy. Hungary lost territory to Czechoslovakia, Romania and Yugoslavia by the Treaty of Trianon (June 1920).

Unfortunately the redrawing of national boundaries caused more problems than it solved.

Shifting powers

Today we think of the idea of **colonies** – countries ruled by other countries who exploit their **natural resources** and population – as being unfair. But until the middle of the 20th century many people, in Britain and France especially, thought colonies were a good thing. They viewed their colonies as important markets for their manufactured goods and as suppliers of cheap **raw materials** for their industries. They also saw their own countries as being superior and therefore entitled to rule over the less developed Asian or African nations.

Declining powers

Britain and France had entered the 20th Century as two of the strongest nations in the world. Much of their wealth and prosperity came from their large **empires**. But the huge cost of World War One had drained this wealth, and by the 1920s and 1930s their empires were costing more to upkeep than they were providing in resources.

Britain had lost most of Ireland in 1922, and the Dominions (Canada, Australia, New Zealand and South Africa), although already self-governing, became fully independent in 1926. **Nationalist** groups, who wanted independence for their own countries, were especially powerful in such imperial possessions as India, Egypt, Iraq and Persia (now Iran). France too was waging a constant struggle against nationalist groups in Indo-China (now Vietnam, Laos and Cambodia), and in French possessions in the Middle East and North Africa.

Up and coming powers

But as Britain and France struggled in the postwar world, other nations grew stronger. Even before World War One the USA was the richest, most powerful country in the world.

Gerrit Beneker's painting of an American construction worker in front of a towering line of skyscrapers, symbolizes the optimism and prosperity of post-war America.

It emerged from the war even stronger. If anyone was capable of challenging the French and British as 'world leaders' it was the USA. But many Americans had not wanted to fight in the war in the first place, and resented the fact that their country had rescued Britain and France and their empires, which many Americans regarded with distaste. A spirit of '**isolationism**' dominated the USA throughout the 1920s and 1930s.

These Russian peasants, photographed in 1921, are victims of a famine brought about by the upheaval of the civil war which followed the 1917 communist revolution.

The **Soviet Union** was another huge country with massive potential and a vast population. Until 1917 it was a nation ruled by a monarchy. Although some industrialization had taken place, the majority of its people still made a living off the land. Many people were **illiterate** and poverty was widespread in both the cities and the rural areas. A **communist revolution** in that year overthrew the old regime, and the next twenty years were spent trying to turn the country into a modern, industrial power. The new regime was also occupied in establishing the authority of the communist government on the country. In the process **civil war**, famine and huge '**purges**', left millions of people dead or imprisoned. Due to this turmoil, the Soviet Union was to play only a minor role in world affairs until 1939.

But there were other ambitious countries like Germany, Italy and Japan. In the two decades following World War One, each would be taken over by regimes whose leaders were determined to make their nations rich and powerful. The aggressive way in which these governments pursued this policy was, as we shall see, one of the main causes of World War Two.

Neville Chamberlain on the British Empire

'*We are a very rich and vulnerable Empire, and there are plenty of poor adventurers not very far away who look upon us with hungry eyes.*'
Neville Chamberlain, British prime minister 1937-40.

Germany in the 1920s

Germany emerged from World War One as a new **democracy**. The new government, was called the Weimar **Republic**, after the German town where the **constitution** was written. It was Germany's first democracy without a monarchy and it came at a time of national humiliation and economic turmoil. The leaders who replaced Germany's military chiefs and monarch were inexperienced politicians. These men, rather than the military generals, were often blamed for the outcome of the Treaty of Versailles. They were also blamed for Germany's economic problems in the 1920s. Extremists such as Hitler found plenty of reasons for blaming Germany's troubles on 'democracy'.

Hard times

Fate had landed Germany's new democratic government with a dreadful set of circumstances. The European victors were determined to make Germany pay for the cost of the war. A popular saying at the time was 'squeeze the German lemon until the pips squeak'. But the European victors also wanted to ensure that Germany would remain too weak in the future to be able to fight in another conflict. It was a harsh and unrealistic hope, and one that caused great hardship in Germany in the 1920s. The problem was obvious. Germany was being forced to pay cripplingly high reparation payments, yet its economy was in tatters.

When Germany failed to make reparation payments in 1923, the French sent their army into the Ruhr, Germany's main industrial region. These soldiers are cycling into the city of Essen.

When Germany was unable to meet reparation payments in 1923, France and Belgium sent troops into Germany's industrial region of the Ruhr to take coal in place of the money owed. This was one occasion, when the vast majority of the German people united behind their Weimar government in protest. It was humiliations such as this that fanned German hatred for its old enemies. After the occupation of the Ruhr, inflation became a particularly damaging problem. The value of money fell so dramatically that many businesses failed and there was mass **unemployment**.

Gradual recovery

By the mid-1920s, Germany and the rest of Europe had begun to recover. The German economy revived and the country settled into a brief four-year period of prosperity. In 1928 the German economy was almost as strong as it had been in 1914, and by the end of the decade, Germany was the second largest exporter of goods in the world, after the USA.

Much of this recovery was due to two economic packages put together by American financiers to help Germany pay their reparations with greater ease. The first, the Dawes Plan (named after Charles G. Dawes) was put into practice in 1924. While this plan did not reduce the amount of debt it did help Germany by making the schedule of payments easier. But the plan proved to be unworkable and was replaced by the Young Plan in 1929 (named after Owen D. Young). Here, total reparation payments were reduced by 75 per cent and were to be paid in 59 annual instalments. (This would have taken them up to 1988.) The first of these payments was made in 1930, but by the next year Germany was once again in economic turmoil. The effects of world-wide economic **depression** had made themselves felt, and Germany could not afford to pay. When Hitler came to power in 1933 he cancelled all subsequent payments.

As Germany's economy collapsed, money lost its value. These German children are playing with worthless German bank notes.

Inflation

This is an economic term. It describes a situation where prices for goods go up dramatically, and the value of money goes down. Wages buy increasingly less than they used to, and savings become less and less valuable. In Germany in the autumn of 1923 inflation was so bad that prices in restaurants were put on blackboards so they could be changed frequently.

The effects of the Great Depression

In the years after World War One the USA had become increasingly prosperous. Then in 1929 the American economy failed disastrously. This was triggered by an event known as the Wall Street Crash, which led to severe and prolonged economic hardship all over the world – an era known as 'The Great **Depression**'. The Wall Street Crash was the name given to the collapse of the American **stock market**, which was based around Wall Street – the USA's financial centre in New York. In the 1920s the stock market had experienced a period of massive expansion, when millions of people had invested in stocks and **shares** in the hope of making quick and easy money. But when stock prices began to fall in late 1929 there was panic selling which had a catastrophic effect on the US economy during the 1930s. People's savings disappeared and businesses ran out of money.

An American investor who has lost his entire savings in the Wall Street Crash tries to make money by selling his car.

The USA suffered considerably, especially in the rural agricultural states. Concern for its own problems led the USA to turn away from world affairs, often against the wishes of the president at the time, Franklin D. Roosevelt, who held the post from 1933 until 1945. He was in a particularly difficult position. To help with the USA's economic recovery he had set up a policy called 'The New Deal', whereby the American government took an active role in creating work and encouraging business. In order to carry through these policies, he had to depend on support from politicians who were strongly in favour of '**isolationism**' – keeping America away from any involvement in foreign affairs.

Global impact

The Great Depression had far-reaching global effects because so many different countries were dependent on the USA's wealth. US factories bought **raw materials** from other countries and US consumers bought goods that were imported from abroad. In addition, huge sums of money were lent by US banks to countries trying to rebuild their war-shattered economies. Now demand for goods suddenly dropped and bank loans were withdrawn. As a result **unemployment** and bankruptcies (a state of financial ruin) rose throughout the world. Countries which had struggled to regain their prosperity after the war now found themselves in dire economic straits once again.

With trade between nations so badly affected, '**protectionism**' flourished. In Britain for example, from 1932 onwards, there was a tendency to trade with the countries of the **empire**, a policy known as 'Imperial Preference'.

Increased economic competition turned into to rivalry and led to growing hostility between nations.

Extreme solutions

All over the world as wages fell, unemployment and desperate poverty rose. In the 1920s and 1930s governments provided very little state aid to help the poor and the unemployed. It is hardly surprising that in such difficult times many people turned to political extremes for a solution. They believed that extreme measures were needed to combat the problems caused by the Great Depression.

In Germany and Japan, which were both severely hit by the Great Depression, **radical**, strongly **nationalistic** political groups gained power. Germany lacked oil and Japan had few **natural resources**. As they needed these to supply their industries, the temptation to take over other countries grew stronger.

*Unemployed German workers queue for state aid during the Great Depression of the early 1930s. Hitler offered men such as these the prospect of work and prosperity. At the same time providing clear scapegoats for their troubles, like the **communists** and the Jews.*

Mussolini and fascist Italy

The years between the wars produced some of the most brutal and ruthless dictators of modern history: Josef Stalin in the **Soviet Union**, Adolf Hitler in Germany, General Franco in Spain and Benito Mussolini in Italy.

Italy had been one of the victorious countries of World War One, but had failed to win the territory it wanted at the end of the war. The country was engulfed in a wave of **strikes** and street fighting between rival political extremists, and the weak, **democratic** government collapsed under the strain.

In the early 1920s Mussolini rose to prominence in Italian politics as leader of a **nationalistic**, **authoritarian** party called the **fascists**. A former **socialist**, he described himself as 'an adventurer for all roads'. This suited his party well, for it was an odd mixture, including extremists, **trade unionists**, **anarchists** and **republicans**.

Mussolini, dressed in full fascist uniform, makes an impassioned speech at an Italian rally in 1934. Like Hitler, he was an impressive public speaker.

The fascists come to power

In 1922, Mussolini announced that his followers would march on Rome to seize control of the country, and save it from lawlessness. Much to everyone's surprise, the Italian King Victor Emmanuel III took this as a cue to invite Mussolini to form a government. This was to avoid a **civil war** or a **communist revolution** similar to the one that had deposed the Russian monarchy in 1917. In 1925 Mussolini turned his rule into a **dictatorship**.

Despite Mussolini's often brutal treatment of political opponents his party was widely popular, and Italy seemed to flourish under fascism. Strikes ended, industry produced more goods, and, as was often said at the time, 'the trains ran on time'. Drastic and dramatic reforms were announced. There would be 'battles' for more land, more grain, more roads and even for a higher birth rate.

Benito Mussolini (1883–1945)

Compared with other dictators, Mussolini seems almost likeable, and it is easy to forget that he ordered opponents to be murdered. Like Hitler, this one-time teacher and journalist owed his success to his great skill as an orator (speech maker). To many people in Italy at this time he seemed like an inspired saviour of his country. Known to Italians as 'Il Duce' (pronounced Eel Doo-chey) 'the leader', he once described his policies as '97 cents worth of mere public clamour and three cents worth of solid achievement.'

Partners in crime: the Italian magazine Il Mattino Illustrato celebrates a visit to Italy by Hitler in 1938 with this montage of the German dictator standing beside Mussolini.

However Mussolini's rule lacked any real substance, and his reforms faltered because of the widespread **corruption** that blossomed as fascist **cronies** seized control of local and national government organizations. As his policies failed at home in Italy, Mussolini increasingly looked to adventures abroad to bolster support for his regime.

Mussolini and Hitler

The German **Nazi** leader Adolf Hitler and Mussolini were fated to be political partners. Their political beliefs were very similar. Both men sought glory and power for their countries through authoritarian government and military conquest. Both dictators would die at the end of the war. However, when Hitler first came to power Mussolini regarded him as a rival, and actively disliked him, once referring to him as a 'mad little clown'. Hitler though, admired the Italian leader greatly, and modelled the Nazis on Mussolini's Fascist Party. For example, the Italian fascists had their own private army of violent ex-soldiers, known as blackshirts. Hitler copied this idea with his own brownshirts. Hitler also adopted other fascist ideas, such as Mussolini's **cult of personality**, his fascist youth organizations and the fascist salute – which Italians were encouraged to make instead of a handshake, because it was 'more hygienic'.

Japan after World War One

During the 19th century people in the **West** were used to thinking of the nations of the Far East as places to trade with or conquer. Japan was an uncommon exception. Japan only opened its ports to Western trade when US Navy commander Matthew Perry arrived with steamship gunboats in 1853. A close-knit, traditional society, Japan soon made use of Western technology, and within half a century had become a modern, industrial nation. Its victory over the Russians in the Russo-Japanese war of 1904–5 announced to the world that it was a confident, strong nation, capable of humiliating one of Europe's largest military powers.

Failing friendships

Japan forged close trade and cultural links with both Britain and the USA, and fought on the side of the **Allies** in World War One. Yet after the war, Japan was not treated as the great power it thought itself to be. At Versailles, the Japanese **delegates** were particularly angry when their European allies were not prepared to recognize the concept of racial equality, and seemed to regard Japan as an inferior country. Then in 1922, the Washington Naval Conference, attempted to limit the size of Japan's navy. It was humiliating for Japan when it was agreed that its navy should be kept smaller than the navies of Britain or the USA. Like many other aspects of their **diplomacy** after World War One, the Allies had made a serious misjudgement. Their arrogant behaviour played a part in turning a friendly nation into a formidable enemy.

Japan already had its own mini-**empire** and had been in control of Korea since 1905. Even after the Washington Naval Conference, Japan had a strong navy. It also had a powerful army led by generals who wanted to see Japan use her military strength to extend Japanese influence in Asia and to protect Japan 'from **socialism**'. After World War One, Japan emerged as the major economic power in eastern and south Asia, but the 1920s and 1930s were to bring difficult times. Japan's prosperity was temporarily disrupted by the 1923 Tokyo earthquake, which flattened the city and left over 140,000 dead. The world-wide **depression** also affected Japan very badly.

Turn to the right

Inside Japan, there was a noticeable shift in political thinking, which was partly due to this economic turmoil. Though Japan had made some progress towards establishing a **democracy**, it was still a very **conservative** society. Japan's military leaders in particular, who had increasingly come to control the country during the 1930s, thought Japan should assert its power and authority over weaker neighbouring countries. These military leaders were also more sympathetic to the **authoritarian** and militaristic ideals of the **fascist** countries of Germany and Italy.

Japan was a powerful industrial nation, but it had few **natural resources** of its own. During the early 1930s, Japan began to suffer from the effects of the depression. The silk industry was badly affected and there was widespread poverty in both the cities and the countryside. Japan's military leaders, thinking that the government was incapable of solving these problems, were preparing to act. They looked towards China and the Far Eastern **colonies** of the European powers such as Britain, France and the Netherlands, who were also struggling with the depression. Here in the Dutch East Indies, Indochina, Malaya and other territories there were resources such as oil and rubber which they believed would bring prosperity to Japan.

This ominous poster from 1937 shows a Japanese boy dressed as a soldier armed with bayonet and rifle, and points the way to Japan's future ambitions in the Asian Pacific.

Japan's military leaders

Many of Japan's politicians were disturbed by the growing influence of the country's military leaders. Koki Hirota, who was prime minister from 1936-37, said: *'The Military are like an untamed horse left to run wild. If you try head-on to stop it, you'll get kicked to death.'*

The rise of Hitler

The years after World War One were very difficult for Germany, but worse was to come. In this troubled atmosphere a particularly gifted politician named Adolf Hitler managed to persuade the German people that only by his strong leadership would Germany's former power and prosperity be restored.

Hitler had first sprung to national attention in the 1920s. After the war this obscure Austrian corporal had been employed by the army to spy on extremist political organizations. As an undercover agent (acting secretly) he was sent to Munich to join a **right-wing nationalist** group called the German Workers' Party. He liked them so much he joined them and within a couple of years he became their president.

The Nazi Party

Hitler gave the group a new name – the National **Socialist** German Workers' Party. It became known as the **Nazi** Party. The Nazi Party called for all German peoples to be united into one nation. They blamed the Jews and the **communists** for Germany's misfortunes and vowed to avenge Germany for the humiliation of the Treaty of Versailles. The Nazis had a distinct identity, with colourful banners and a swastika symbol.

Inspired by Mussolini's 'March on Rome' the Nazi Party led by Hitler intended to topple the Weimar Government in a similar way. In November 1923, at a time of mass **unemployment**, **strikes**, and street fighting between rival political groups, Hitler and a group of armed Nazi thugs burst into a government meeting in a Munich beer hall. Here they announced they were going to set up a national government. But police fired on the Nazis as they marched towards the Bavarian War Ministry, and Hitler was arrested and sent to prison for eight months. After this he decided that the way to power was through the conventional route of winning an election. But as Germany began to recover from the war and her economy prospered, Nazi support slumped dramatically.

Hitler salutes his supporters during a Nazi rally in 1927. Ceremonies such as this raised the profile of the Nazis, and served to intimidate their political enemies.

Hitler's come-back

The Great **Depression** brought Hitler to power. In 1928 the Nazi vote was a mere 800,000 – 2.6 per cent of the population. Yet by July of 1932, when the effects of the depression were being felt, it had risen to 13,750,000 – 37.3 per cent. Hitler's Nazi Party appealed to many sections of German society. Powerful business people and industrialists thought he would protect their country from a communist **revolution**, and made generous donations to his party. Ordinary, often unemployed, Germans began to feel that Hitler was the only politician capable of leading their country out of economic ruin. Like Mussolini, he was a hypnotically powerful speaker, and soon thousands, then millions, of Germans fell under his spell.

By January 1933, the Nazis held the greatest number of seats in the Reichstag – the German parliament – but they did not have a majority. A partnership with Chancellor Franz von Papen's Catholic Centre Party brought them to power. Once in office, they swiftly ditched their political **allies**, and took total control of Germany.

Once in power, Nazi hatred of the Jews became official state policy. Here, in April 1933, Nazi officials in Berlin place a notice on the window of a Jewish clothes shop, urging their fellow Germans not to shop there.

Mein Kampf

Hitler presented his evil philosophy in a book entitled *Mein Kampf* (My Struggle) which was published in 1925. Here are some of its main points:

- Hitler would lead the Aryan race (broadly meaning people of 'pure' German blood) in a war to enslave the inferior Slavs of eastern Europe and Russia.

- The land they conquered would become '*Lebensraum*' (living space) for the German people.

- The communist **Soviet Union** was Germany's greatest enemy and must be destroyed.

- The Jews were the greatest enemy of mankind and were to be 'eliminated'.

Hitler's Germany

Once in power, Hitler began to transform Germany, turning his extreme ideas into a living reality with remarkable speed. All aspects of daily life were put under the control of the **Nazi** Party – from newspapers and radio broadcasts, to schools and universities. The German people were bombarded with Nazi **propaganda** from every angle. School children, for example, said prayers of thanks to Hitler, rather than God, and were encouraged to play 'Jews and Aryans' rather than 'Cowboys and Indians'. Those who were brave enough to oppose the new regime faced the prospect of arrest by the feared *Gestapo* (the Nazi secret police) and execution, or imprisonment in brutal **concentration camps**. The first of the permanent concentration camps was set up in Germany in 1933, soon after Hitler came to power.

A Nazi rally in Nuremburg in 1933. Rallies were seen to be a way of uniting the German people behind the Nazi cause.

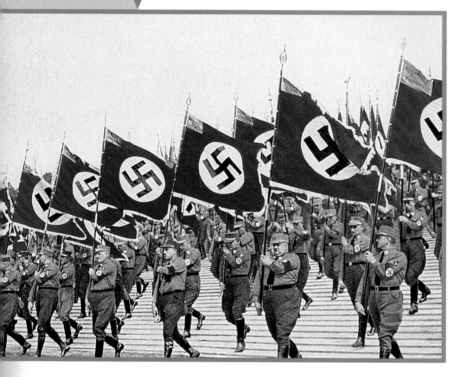

Germany rearms

Unemployment had been one of Germany's greatest problems during the early years of the 1930s, so one of the Nazis' first tasks was to put the German people back to work. They did this by commissioning a series of public works – most notably Germany's *autobahn* (motorway) system. Schemes such as this put millions of people back to work, and by 1939 unemployment in Germany had been virtually eliminated.

Like almost everything else the Nazis did, however, the motorway building had a hidden purpose – it made the movement of troops and military equipment through Germany much easier. In 1933 Hitler told his chief ministers: 'The next five years must be dedicated to the rearmament of the German people. Every publicly supported work-creation scheme must be judged from this standpoint: is it necessary for the restoration of the military strength of the German people?' Over five years government armament spending increased by 70 per cent. Much of Germany's workforce had been put back to work to produce tanks, battleships, submarines and warplanes.

Preparing the people for war

Hitler boasted that his regime (which was known as 'The Third Reich') would last for a thousand years. To prepare for the wars which were intended to turn Germany into a global power, German children had to be readied for the struggle to come. In 1936 a law was passed proclaiming: 'The future of the German people depends on its youth. The entire German youth must therefore be prepared for its future duties.' All German children had to join an organization called the Hitler Youth, for boys, and for girls the League of German Maidens. Here their minds were further stoked with Nazi ideas about the superiority of the German race, and the evils of **communism** and the Jews. The Hitler Youth concentrated on developing physical fitness and military skills to prepare boys for life as soldiers. In the League of German Maidens girls were taught that their greatest role in life was to have as many children as possible, to provide Hitler with soldiers for his army.

These German girls are members of the League of German Maidens. Hitler had a low opinion of women, and saw them mainly as providers of soldiers for his armies. By turning children into good Nazis Hitler hoped to increase his power.

Adolf Hitler (1889–1945)

The son of a customs official, Hitler was born in Austria and grew up wanting to be an artist. His beliefs about the German 'master race', and his hatred of the Jews, were shared by many in the Austrian capital of Vienna, where Hitler lived as a homeless drifter before World War One. During the war Hitler served as a corporal on the Western Front. He loved army life, and was twice awarded the Iron Cross medal for bravery. The defeat of Germany in the war, and the Versailles peace treaty that followed it, filled Hitler with a lasting hatred for Germany's enemies, and the 'traitors' in the German government who he felt had betrayed his country.

The Soviet Union between the wars

Of all the great powers involved in World War One, it was Russia that suffered the most. Russia's ill-equipped troops fought many long and disastrous campaigns that left over half the country's fighting forces dead or injured. By 1917, the huge Russian **empire** had collapsed into anarchy, the monarchy was toppled, and within a few months the **Bolshevik** Party, led by Vladimir Illyich Lenin, seized power.

A humiliating peace treaty with Germany at Brest-Litovsk was signed by the new **communist** leaders in 1918, by which Russia lost large amounts of territory on both her western and southern borders. This was followed by a bitter **civil war** between the new government and anti-communist forces aided by troops from Britain, France and the USA. The war, and the famine that accompanied it, claimed the lives of millions of Russians. It ended in victory for the communist government, and the country was renamed the USSR (Union of Soviet **Socialist Republics**).

The leaders of the **Soviet Union** had hoped that further communist revolutions would sweep through Europe. When this failed to happen they turned their efforts to strengthening the world's first communist nation.

Dictator Josef Stalin (fourth from left) with fellow leaders of the Soviet Union in 1929. Within a decade almost all these men would fall victim to Stalin's infamous purges.

Stalin takes control

By January 1924 Lenin was dead. After a power struggle, the control of this huge nation finally passed to Josef Stalin in 1928. Further suffering was brought upon the Russian people as sweeping agricultural and industrial reforms were carried out. Millions died in further famines and in terrifying '**purges**', where anyone suspected of being an enemy of communism was executed, or sent to labour camps (places where people were often worked to death) in the desolate northern region of Siberia in eastern Russia.

In the 1930s Stalin watched with alarm the rise of Hitler in Germany. The **Nazis** were sworn enemies of communism. Japanese intentions too, on Russia's south-eastern border, were a another anxiety. Yet Stalin weakened his position even further when a devastating purge of the Russian military was carried out during 1937–38. This resulted in almost the entire senior officer corps being replaced by inexperienced but loyal communists. This further undermined the strength of Soviet defences.

Looking for friends

The Soviet Union searched for **allies** against the Nazis, but their regime was distrusted by almost every government in the world. Leading British politician Winston Churchill, for example, had referred to the Soviet Union as 'this sullen, sinister Bolshevik state'. **Western** nations were unwilling to commit to an **alliance** with the communist regime. So the Soviet Union entered the late 1930s with her army in utter disarray and Nazi Germany glowering on her western frontier. The Russian people had already endured twenty years of terror and hardship, and now an ordeal of even greater calamity awaited them. But first, there would be a bizarre twist to the tale as two sworn enemies became allies.

Supervised by Red Army soldiers, thousands of Soviet workers troop through Moscow's central Red Square during the 1929 May Day rally celebrating the communist revolution.

Josef Stalin (1879–1953)

Russia's leader from 1928, Stalin was one of the most cruel and feared **dictators** in history. Using the Soviet secret police to enforce his rule, his attempts to modernize Soviet Russia brought massive hardship to his people. Yet Stalin was also adored by many Russians, mainly because Soviet **propaganda** portrayed him as a god-like ruler, but also because his ruthless leadership, at least in part, helped save the Russian people from being conquered and enslaved by the Nazis. His character is tellingly illustrated by a remark he made in 1935 to an aide concerned at the Pope's reaction to the ill treatment of Catholics in the Soviet Union. 'The Pope?' spluttered Stalin, querying the Catholic leader's military strength, 'How many divisions has he got?'

Franco and Spain

In 1936 a **left-wing** Popular Front coalition (mixture of political parties) came to power in Spain, one of the most **conservative**, Catholic countries in Europe. The Popular Front drew its support from mainly working-class voters, and a diverse collection of Spanish **radicals** – **republicans**, **socialists**, **communists**, even **anarchists**. There were also separatist Catalans and Basques who wanted to be independent from Spain. Such a government was too much to bear for Spain's deeply conservative army who rebelled against their new leaders. The rebels came under the leadership of General Francisco Franco, and were supported by the Catholic Church, most of the country's middle class, and Spain's **fascist** party the Falangists. The resulting **civil war**, which was to last until 1939, became a battleground between the two political extremes of communism and fascism. The government side were known as the Republicans, and Franco's rebels were known as the **Nationalists**.

*Spain's **right-wing** leader General Franco is carried on the shoulders of some of his Nationalist soldiers in 1937. Within two years his Nationalist troops had overwhelmed the Republican opposition.*

Friends in low places

Franco's anti-communist sympathies meant he had much in common with Hitler and Mussolini, and both Germany and Italy lent him their support. Hitler sent tanks and aircraft and 10,000 or so men to drive, fly and maintain these war machines. Germany's aircraft, the so-called 'Condor Legion' of 100 planes, were especially effective, and greatly superior to the airforce of the Republicans. They guaranteed the Nationalists control of the skies, making it easier for their armies to advance without fear of attack from above. Not to be outdone, Mussolini sent 50,000 troops from the Italian army.

The Republicans had no help at all from the governments of their fellow **democracies** in **Western** Europe. Instead they made do with 40,000 volunteers from Europe and the USA for the 'International Brigades'. These were made up of left-wing idealists and opponents of fascism. The

Republicans though, did receive help from the **Soviet Union**, who sent tanks and aircraft. The war lasted two years and eventually Franco's better equipped and better organized Nationalists swept the Republicans from power. Altogether about a million people died in the conflict.

Taking sides

Italy, Germany and the Soviet Union, had involved themselves in the Spanish civil war in the hope of winning an **ally** in south-west Europe.

But after his victory, Franco was to prove a disappointment to the fascist **dictators**. Although he offered them goodwill, he cleverly kept his country out of World War Two and because of this, Spain was able to avoid further devastation. By keeping Spain out of World War Two, Franco was also able to ensure that his country would remain a fascist dictatorship until his death in 1975.

This photograph shows the ruined city of Guernica after heavy bombing by German warplanes. Bombing of civilian targets during the Spanish Civil War caused great unease in European cities.

Guernica

One of Hitler's motives for sending military help to the Nationalists in Spain was to give his army and airforce first-hand experience of waging war. The German airforce especially, found the war an ideal training ground for their pilots. In 1937 they carried out one of the most infamous attacks of the conflict. The Basque capital of Guernica was bombed severely with heavy loss of civilian life. The bombing shocked the world, both in its demonstration of fascist ruthlessness, and as an example of the terrible destruction that aircraft could bring to cities and their inhabitants. The effectiveness of the bombing of civilian targets caused great anxiety among Western Europe's city dwellers. It also strengthened support for the British and French policy of trying to avoid war at all costs.

Japan's ambitions for empire

Japanese soldiers march into the Chinese province of Manchuria. The barbaric behaviour of such troops towards China's civilian population caused widespread revulsion throughout the world.

In the 1930s Japan began to take giant strides in her quest to become the great power of the Asian Pacific. Over the Sea of Japan, on the Asian mainland, lay the Chinese province of Manchuria. Japan had long regarded China as a natural **sphere of influence** but had had to compete with other powers, notably Britain and the USA, who also saw China as a market for their goods. The **Soviet Union** too, was wary of Japan's ambitions in China. As the Soviet Union and China shared a common border, the Soviets did not want an expansionist, hostile Japan on their doorstep.

In the 1920s and 1930s China was in a state of political chaos. Rival warlords (local military commanders), the **communist** rebels and the government of Jiang Jieshi (also spelt Chiang Kai-Shek), all competed for control of this huge country. Japan's increasingly aggressive military leaders decided conditions were perfect for a takeover. So, in 1931, Japanese troops poured into Manchuria in northern China. After a short campaign, they conquered the region. The territory, which was renamed Manchukuo, would stay in Japanese hands until the end of World War Two.

It was a well-calculated risk. The Soviet Union, wrapped up in its own internal problems, did nothing. The League of Nations protested, but without an army and the full support of member countries, there was little else it could do. Britain and the USA were angry, but split over who should confront Japan.

Japan grows bolder

In 1934, the Japanese government formulated the Amau doctrine, which officially declared that China was within Japan's sphere of influence. In 1936, an army revolt in Japan put the military firmly in charge of the government, and Japan grew bolder still. In 1937, Japan launched an attack into China which became an all–

out war. At first Japanese armies met with great success. In January 1938, Jiang Jieshi's capital city Nanjing fell, and the world witnessed the appalling spectacle of the Japanese Imperial Army laying waste to the city. More than 100,000 people were killed in an orgy of rape, looting and murder. The massacre was in fact carefully calculated to frighten Japan's neighbours, so they would not be tempted to resist any future attack.

By 1937 the war in the Far East had spread into the rest of China. These Japanese armoured cars are driving through the streets of Shanghai.

Further conquests ...

Japan was now set on a course which saw her determined to confront the older **colonial** powers of Britain, France and the Netherlands in Asia. Japan's leaders correctly guessed however, that their main rival for domination of the Asian Pacific was actually the USA. The European powers had their own problems to contend with and their colonies would be easy to overcome. The USA would be more difficult to defeat.

Japan's claim to be master of Asia

Japan had many pressing reasons for wanting to expand her territory and influence in Pacific Asia. She was a small and already overcrowded country with a rapidly growing population. Before World War One both the USA and Australia had been popular destinations for Japanese people wishing to emigrate. By the 1930s both these countries refused to allow more Japanese people to settle there. Although Japan had a powerful industrial base, it had few **natural resources**. Japan's leaders felt they had as much right as any other country to become a colonial power and from 1940 onwards promoted this policy with the **propaganda** slogan 'Asia for Asians'. However, as a conquering colonial power, Japan was just as exploitative and often considerably crueller than the European powers she replaced.

Italy's new Roman Empire

International relations throughout the 1930s were dominated by aggressive **right-wing** regimes challenging the existing world order. Japan invaded China. Germany, as we shall see, challenged and overturned the borders imposed by the Treaty of Versailles. In Italy, Mussolini's domestic policies began to falter and so he turned to foreign adventures to distract the Italian people from the failures of his regime.

Adventures in Africa

Italy had a glorious imperial past – the Roman **Empire** had once ruled over most of the known world. Mussolini dreamed of creating a new Italian empire to rival the old. Italy had some **colonial** possessions in Africa, notably Libya, Eritrea and Italian Somaliland, which shared a border with Abyssinia (now called Ethiopia). This mountainous African kingdom was one of the few independent nations left on the continent – most of the rest having been colonized by other European powers. Abyssinia, Mussolini believed, would be a good place to start – especially as the country had close trading links with Italy.

Protected by his imperial guard, the Abyssinian Emperor Haile Selassie is pictured here shortly after his country's invasion by the Italian army in 1935.

The League of Nations

This international organization had been set up after World War One to solve disputes between nations by peaceful means. Its members were committed to open **diplomacy** and were bound by an understanding that they would abide by the League's mutually agreed decisions. As a final resort, members of the League could impose economic **sanctions** on any country whose actions they disapproved of. Without support from the USA and with no military force of its own, the League was powerless against any determinedly aggressive nation. The actions of Italy, Japan and Germany in the 1930s totally undermined its credibility.

Mussolini calculated that the poorly equipped Abyssinian army would be easy to defeat, and in October 1935 he attacked them with 300,000 troops armed with the advanced weapons of 20th-century warfare. Despite the poison gas and aerial bombardment they were subjected to, the barefoot soldiers, of the Emperor Haile Selassie managed to hold off the Italians for a whole eight months before the capital city, Addis Ababa, fell to Italian forces in May 1936.

European reaction

The **Western** European powers reacted with dismay. The League of Nations protested. But there was no will to take any determined action. Britain and France especially, were determined not to drive Mussolini into a closer partnership with Hitler. Nevertheless their muted disapproval proved an incentive for Mussolini to do just that. In 1936 Germany and Italy announced they had formed an '**Axis**' (hub) around which, they grandly announced, 'all European states can also assemble'.

Mussolini's empire building began with the invasion of Abyssinia in 1935–36. By 1941 Italy was forced to give up its African colonies of Eritrea and Somaliland, and Abyssinian independence was restored.

A troubled partnership
History depicts Hitler and Mussolini as firm friends and close **allies**. But this was not always the case. When they first met in 1934 Mussolini described Hitler as a 'barbarian'. Italy objected fiercely to an early Nazi attempt to seize Austria in 1934, and initially saw Germany as a rival for influence in the Balkan region of south-eastern Europe. When they did become close allies, Germany's friendship with Italy would do Hitler few favours.

Mussolini hoped to inspire his people to be more warlike with the slogan, 'Better to be a lion for a day than a sheep for 100 years.' But his real problem was that the Italian people had no appetite for war. It was his own desperate desire for glory that would bring Italy into World War Two on the side of the **Nazis**, and lead both himself and his country to destruction.

Hitler tests the water

If Hitler felt history had been cruel to Germany in 1918, then he could hardly complain in the 1930s. The decade was a perfect time for someone with his vision of Germany's future to push the boundaries and see what he could get away with. The USA was pursuing its policy of **isolationism**. The **Soviet Union** was preoccupied with establishing its own brand of **communism**. Britain and France were so keen to reach an understanding with Hitler he must have thought they would let him get away with anything.

Germany was gathering **allies** too. After initial hostility from Italy, Mussolini was drawing closer to the **Nazis**. The Japanese, seeing Nazi Germany as an enemy of the Soviet Union, joined an anti-Communist agreement with Germany in 1936. Italy joined a year later. The agreement was called the Anti-Comintern Pact. All three powers had a desire to redraw the map of the world in a way that suited them better.

Soon after Hitler came to power in Germany in 1933 he set about rearming the nation. This picture shows a German aircraft factory producing Heinkel bombers which were later used to bomb European cities.

Plans for world domination

But while Japan and Italy just wanted to expand their **colonial** possessions, Germany had ambitions that were far greater. Hitler wanted his country to rule the world. He saw the achievement of this aim as a two-stage plan. Firstly Germany was to regain the territory lost at the Treaty of Versailles, and also take over territory in Europe. When Germany controlled *mitteleuropa* (central and eastern Europe) it would have access to coal, iron ore, oil and a workforce to build a war machine capable of taking Hitler's plan to stage two.

At stage two he intended to build an **empire** to the east of Germany to provide *Lebensraum* (living space) for his German master race. This, in effect, meant the conquest of Poland and European Russia. Once these territories had been incorporated, Germany would be the strongest power on earth.

> **GERMANY PREPARES FOR WAR**
> THE FIGURES BELOW SHOW THE AMOUNT AND THE PROPORTION OF GERMANY'S NATIONAL INCOME THAT WAS SPENT ON ARMAMENTS FROM THE YEAR HITLER GAINED POWER, TO THE YEAR WORLD WAR TWO BEGAN.
>
> 1933 2% (1.2 MILLION REICHMARKS)
> 1936 11% (10.2 MILLION REICHMARKS)
> 1939 30% (38 MILLION REICHMARKS)

Step one and onwards

Almost as soon as he gained power, Hitler started to rearm Germany. After World War One, as part of the Treaty of Versailles, an area of land known as the Saar (see map page 9) was put under the control of the League of Nations. In 1935 this coal-rich region voted to return to Germany. Then, from 1936, Hitler began to carry through stage one of his masterplan. In March of that year German troops entered the demilitarized Rhineland – the common border with France. Protests against this violation of the Treaty of Versailles were made, but no direct action was taken by France or Britain. It was commonly said in Britain that Hitler was 'only marching into his own backyard'.

In March 1938 German troops entered Austria, and the country was united with Germany – another move strictly forbidden by the treaty. Again no action was taken. Then Hitler turned his attention to another part of eastern Europe. This was the Sudetenland (see map page 9) in Czechoslovakia, home to some 3 million German-speakers. Certain that Germany would have to fight to regain this territory Hitler's generals were instructed to prepare their armies for war. Meanwhile, France and Britain had been watching Germany's growing strength with increasing alarm, and they chose this moment to intervene.

Hitler makes a triumphant entry into Vienna, the capital city of Austria, following the country's union with Germany in March 1938.

Anschluss

The *Anschluss* was the name given to the unification of Germany and Austria. This event took place in March of 1938. Austria already had a strong Nazi movement of its own and when Hitler sent his troops into Austria many people came out of their homes to welcome them.

Appeasement and Munich

In the inter-war years Britain and France were two of the greatest powers in Europe. But by 1938 Germany had, once again, turned into a major rival. The **Nazis** were openly rearming and had demonstrated the effectiveness of their tanks and warplanes in the Spanish **Civil War**. The Saar, the Rhineland and Austria had all been fully incorporated into the Reich (the German state). Now Hitler had begun to demand the Sudetenland. Hitler had considerable support among the German-speaking Sudetenlanders, most of whom were happy to be united with Germany.

Ill-prepared

The British and French prime ministers, Neville Chamberlain and Edouard Daladier, were faced with an awkward situation. Both were keen to protect their country's power and prestige, and not to allow Hitler to bully them. But both were compromised. Their armed forces were ill-prepared for a war. Their people did not want a war – the memory of the dreadful slaughter of World War One was still fresh in their minds. Additionally, British and French leaders both recognized that Germany had been badly treated by the Treaty of Versailles and felt therefore that Germany had the right to correct this situation. Also there was considerable support for **fascism** in France, and many upper-class British people had a sneaking admiration for Hitler. Both countries saw the Nazis, and fascist Italy, as potential **allies** against the **communist Soviet Union**.

Hitler, when the occasion demanded, could appear warm and charming. Here he greets British Prime Minister Chamberlain with a friendly smile during one of their meetings at Munich in September 1938.

All these various strands came together in a policy known as '**appeasement**'. But appeasement assumed that Britain and France were allowing Hitler to redraw the map of Europe on terms that were acceptable to all three nations.

Hitler resented this attitude, but was clever enough to take advantage of it. As his army prepared to invade Czechoslovakia to annex the Sudetenland, Chamberlain and Daladier, supported by Mussolini, requested

a meeting with Hitler. All four leaders met at Munich. Here, in September 1938, it was agreed that the Sudetenland would be given to Germany. In return, Hitler promised this was 'the last territorial claim I have to make in Europe.'

Peace in our time

History has not been kind to Chamberlain and Daladier. They are remembered as gullible fools who were tricked by a wily Hitler. Maybe they were, but at the time their policy of appeasement was widely popular. Daladier was greeted by a crowd of half a million people when he returned to Paris. The return of Chamberlain to London, clutching a signed agreement from Hitler and declaring 'it is peace in our time', provoked widespread jubilation.

Seen from the present, appeasement had its advantages. In practical terms, there was little Britain or France could do to help Czechoslovakia. Besides, by delaying war with Germany, Chamberlain gave Britain more time to rearm – a vital factor in Germany's failure to defeat Britain when war finally came.

The German occupation of Prague in March 1939 caused great anger in the streets of the Czech capital, but little real resistance.

Appeasement in the Far East

The British government also applied the policy of appeasement to Japan. They recognized that Japan was a powerful nation which deserved some measure of influence over its neighbouring countries in Asia. Japan's occupation of Manchuria was accepted, partly because the British thought a powerful Japan would prevent the Soviet Union from extending its communist influence into Asia. The fact that there was very little Britain could do about Japanese aggression also aided this acceptance.

Europeans who took the Munich agreement at face value slept soundly in their beds for a few more months. Then, in March 1939, Nazi soldiers marched into the rest of Czechoslovakia. Few now doubted that war could be avoided. In the summer of 1939 Nazi Germany turned its attention to Poland. The continent held its breath and waited for the spark that would ignite another war.

The Nazi-Soviet Pact

Throughout the 1930s the **Soviet Union** had been regarded with fear and distrust by both the **Western democracies** and the **right-wing dictatorships** of Europe. However, as war loomed at the end of the decade, leaders on all sides pondered the benefits of an **alliance** with the world's only **communist** nation.

A failed alliance

In March 1939 German soldiers marched into Prague, and claimed the western half of Czechoslovakia as their own. The agreement Germany had made with Britain and France at Munich had obviously failed. A month later, the Soviet Union suggested an alliance with Britain and France against Germany. The proposal was met with only lukewarm interest. Britain hoped for support against Germany from other countries in eastern Europe, particularly Poland. Poland especially, feared that the Soviet Union wanted to win back land lost after World War One.

Talks between Britain, France and the Soviet Union continued over the summer, but France and Britain deliberately delayed any final commitment. Britain, for example, sent only minor officials, who had no real power to make decisions, to the Soviet Union to negotiate. They travelled by boat, rather than plane, so they took weeks to get there. Eventually, Britain and France decided the Soviet Union was too unreliable, and they could do without its support. The talks ground to a halt in August 1939.

David Low's classic illustration of Hitler and Stalin greeting each other with cordial insults over the body of a Polish soldier. This cartoon perfectly captures the utter disbelief many people felt on hearing of the Nazi-Soviet Pact.

Germany steps in

Meanwhile, **Nazi** foreign minister Joachim von Ribbentrop had also approached his Soviet counterpart Vyacheslav Molotov. When talks with the Western democracies failed Molotov agreed to meet Ribbentrop. Ribbentrop knew the Nazis planned to invade Poland at any moment and therefore was particularly keen to make an agreement. Hitler sent a telegram to Stalin, who replied within two hours. Ribbentrop

The Nazi-Soviet Pact

- The Nazis and Soviets would not attack each other.
- Russia would supply Germany with **raw materials**, in return for weapons.
- Germany agreed that the Soviets should gain control of Finland, the Baltic States and east Poland.
- The Soviets agreed that Germany should gain control of west Poland.

flew to Moscow, and in the early hours of 24 August 1939, a treaty was agreed in which both countries promised not to attack each other.

Many people were surprised and bewildered when they heard the news that the Nazis and Soviets had signed a non-aggression pact. After all they were known to despise each other's political regimes. In fact, it suited them both, at least for the time being. Hitler wanted to avoid a simultaneous war on Germany's east and west frontiers, as this had considerably hindered the success of Germany in World War One. The Soviets, for their part, were unprepared for war – their army was still recovering from the effects of Stalin's latest **purge**.

Nazi and Soviet troops meet up for a friendly chat in late September 1939, following each country's occupation of sections of Poland.

Europe is mine

When he heard news that the treaty had been agreed, Hitler gloated, 'Now Europe is mine.' Nothing, it seemed, could stop him invading Poland, and with the Soviets' agreement, he was sure that France and Britain would not intervene. Referring to Chamberlain and Daladier he sneered, 'They are little worms. I saw them in Munich. I'll cook them a stew they'll choke on.' Orders for the long-imagined invasion of Poland were put into motion, and Germany's soldiers and tanks headed east to the border.

War breaks out

Germany's seizure of the rest of Czechoslovakia in March 1939, marked the end of **appeasement**. Hitler had humiliated Britain and France. Both countries were now determined not to allow this to happen again. Hitler failed to understand this. Instead, he thought that Poland was of no more significance to the **Western democracies** than Czechoslovakia. The 1938 Czechoslovakian crisis had, after all, been publicly described by Prime Minister Chamberlain as 'a quarrel in a faraway country between people of whom we know nothing'.

Hitler failed to understand that France and Britain did not look on his invasion of Poland in isolation. Instead his rivals saw the invasion as Germany going one step too far. France and Britain now felt they had little option but to stop Germany becoming too powerful in Europe. In 1939 the military balance between the three countries was about even – that is, their military forces were of similar strength. If Germany was allowed to take over Poland without a fight, she would become much stronger than her opponents. Besides, earlier in the year Britain and France had given Poland guarantees that they would attack Germany if Poland was invaded. In expectation of this both France and Britain had begun preparing for war.

Ready to fight

By 1939, Britain especially, was better prepared to fight than she had been at the time of the Munich agreement a year earlier. In April 1939, **conscription** was introduced to bring the armed forces up to wartime strength. New weapons too were now in service – especially fast monoplanes such as Hurricanes and Spitfires. Work was also underway on developing sophisticated radar technology, which could spot approaching enemy aircraft hundreds of kilometres away.

So, when German troops poured over the Polish border, Britain and France both issued ultimatums (final warnings) calling on Germany to withdraw. When these were ignored, Hitler found himself, on 3 September 1939, at war with the world's two greatest **empires**. Only after the event did he realize how badly he had underestimated his enemies' determination to fight. He had spent the last four years taking huge risks, but this time he had overreached himself.

This painting shows a squadron of Spitfires attacking German Heinkel bombers during the Battle of Britain in 1940. Germany's failure to defeat the Royal Air Force saved Britain from invasion.

Map labels:
N W E S compass
ICELAND
NORWAY
SWEDEN
FINLAND
North Sea
Northern Ireland (Part of Britain)
EIRE
BRITAIN
London
DENMARK
ESTONIA
LATVIA
LITHUANIA
East Prussia (Part of Germany)
SOVIET UNION
Atlantic Ocean
NETHERLANDS
Berlin
BELGIUM
GERMANY
LUXEMBOURG
POLAND
Paris
FRANCE
Vichy France
SLOVAKIA
SWITZERLAND AUSTRIA HUNGARY
RUMANIA
Caspian Sea
PORTUGAL
SPAIN
ITALY
Corsica
Sardinia
YUGOSLAVIA
BULGARIA
Black Sea
ALBANIA
GREECE
TURKEY
IRAN
Spanish Morocco
MOROCCO (French)
ALGERIA (French)
TUNISIA (French)
Sicily
Mediterranean Sea
Crete
Cyprus
SYRIA
IRAQ
KUWAIT
PALESTINE
TRANSJORDAN
Neutral Zones
QATAR
km 500
miles 500
LIBYA (Italian)
EGYPT (British Protectorate)
SAUDI ARABIA

Legend:
Axis nations
Nations and areas controlled by Axis Powers
Allied nations occupied by Axis Powers
Nations and areas controlled by Soviet Union
Allied nations occupied by Soviet Union
Allied nations and nations and areas under Allied control
Neutral nations
Vichy France and nations under Vichy control

Nazi victories

At first, everything went Hitler's way. Poland crumbled before Germany's powerful army and its devastating *blitzkrieg* tactics. The following year Hitler turned his attention north and west, and quickly overran Denmark and Norway, Belgium, the Netherlands and Luxembourg. By June of 1940 the German army occupied Paris. It was at this point that Mussolini brought Italy into the war spreading the fighting to the eastern Mediterranean and North Africa. Only Britain lay undefeated in the west, and only because the channel provided a natural barrier that was difficult for armies to cross.

Here Hitler met his first defeat. To carry off a successful invasion of Britain he had to win control of the skies. The Battle of Britain, fought by the Royal Air Force (RAF) against the **Nazi** *Luftwaffe*, was Hitler's first defeat. In a close-fought battle Germany's warplanes were narrowly defeated by the RAF's more speedy and manoeuvrable Hurricanes and Spitfires. With the rest of Europe at his feet Hitler turned instead to his next great project – the invasion of the **Soviet Union**. It would be his greatest mistake.

*Europe 1940. The **Axis** powers controlled much of Europe by this time. The Germans occupied northern France while southern France was put under the control of a new (Vichy) government which supported the Axis powers. The following year Hungary, Romania and Bulgaria joined the Axis.*

From European war to world war

Hitler had not originally planned to attack the **Soviet Union** before the middle of the 1940s, but by 1941 he had conquered large areas of mainland Europe. Germany's position was made even stronger by the Tripartite Pact which had been signed by Germany, Italy and Japan in September 1940. Hungary, Romania, Slovakia and Bulgaria joined them in the spring of 1941. After the fall of France, Hitler declared 'I shall go down in history as the greatest German of them all,' and brought forward plans to invade the Soviet Union.

Despite his optimism Hitler had some unresolved problems. Britain was undefeated, and Hitler's **ally**, Mussolini, was proving to be a hindrance.

This picture shows Soviet troops pushing a piece of anti-tank artillery through a snowy field during the Battle of Moscow in 1941.

Before the planned invasion of the Soviet Union could go ahead in the late spring of 1941, German troops had to be diverted to Africa, the Balkans and Greece to help out Italian armies that were struggling. Towards the end of the war Hitler admitted 'It is in fact quite obvious that our Italian **alliance** has been of more service to our enemies than to ourselves.'

As a result the invasion of the Soviet Union was postponed for a vital month, leaving the German armies with less time to overrun the Soviet Union before the autumn rains slowed down the fighting, and the harsh winter brought it to a standstill.

When the invasion (code named 'Barbarossa') finally came, on 22 June 1941, it was initially an astounding success. Hitler had predicted that the 'rotten' Soviet regime would rapidly collapse. By the autumn advanced units of the German army were already at the gates of Moscow, the nation's capital city. But the Russians bravely fought back. Twenty million of its citizens would die defeating the **Nazis** (on average around 19,000 a day). Hitler's dream of world conquest turned into a nightmare on the vast open plains and mud and snow of Soviet Russia.

War in the Pacific

The invasion of the Soviet Union widened the war's scope, but it was the Japanese who turned World War Two into a truly global conflict. Germany's **Axis** partner Japan took full advantage of the German conquest of France by occupying French Indochina (now Vietnam, Laos and Cambodia) in 1940. Britain and the USA had already responded to Japan's aggressive military policies by imposing an embargo (a ban) on iron and oil exports destined for Japan. The need to seize new sources of these vital **raw materials** before their own stockpiles ran out, led Japan's military leaders to decisive action.

Japanese expansion in the Pacific 1931–42.

Japan's most powerful rival in the Pacific was the USA. So a surprise attack on America's main military base in the Pacific – Pearl Harbor, Hawaii – was planned. Carried out with complete surprise on 7 December 1941, it was a stunning blow. While the USA reeled, Japan carried through an audacious and immensely successful campaign, attacking both American and European possessions. By the middle of 1942, Japan's armies controlled the entire Asian Pacific rim, from the tip of the Aleutian Islands through to Hong Kong, the Philippines, Singapore, Burma and down to Java and New Guinea.

The Pearl Harbor attack had other dramatic consequences. Hitler, drunk on his successes in Europe, declared war on the USA. Finally awakened out of **neutrality** the USA declared war on Japan and then on Japan's allies in Europe. The US turned her hugely powerful economy to winning the war. Within a couple of years her factories would be producing one new warplane every five minutes. Against such military might, the forces of Germany and Japan didn't really stand a chance.

A gloomy future?

Admiral Yamamoto, the architect of the Pearl Harbor attack, responded to praise for its success with the prophetic words *'I fear we have only succeeded in awakening a sleeping tiger.'*

Learning the lessons

'I did so hope that we were going to escape these tragedies. But I sincerely believe that with that madman it was impossible.' So wrote Neville Chamberlain about his struggle to restrain Hitler. Was World War Two inevitable? The answer is probably yes. World War One had ended in a vengeful treaty that was dismissed by one French general as 'a twenty year cease-fire'. Most importantly, in some of the countries where economic hardship brought desperate times, especially during the Great **Depression**, **authoritarian** regimes were able to seize power. The worst of these regimes was led by Hitler. His agenda – to make Germany *the* global power, to destroy **communism** and the Jewish race, as well as to conquer land in eastern Europe – could not fail to bring him into conflict with other nations. Mussolini's desire to create a new Italian **empire** and Japan's wish to dominate Pacific Asia brought conflict to North Africa, China and much of Asia.

Looking back from the present we might wonder if events would have turned out differently if the League of Nations had not been so weak, or Britain and France had not adopted the policy of **appeasement**, or if the USA had turned away from **isolationism** earlier. Perhaps, then, it would not have taken a world war, and all the suffering that caused, to dislodge these **dictators** from power.

Consequences of the war

As the war progressed, the conquering armies of the **Axis** powers were pushed back to their home countries. Hitler committed suicide and Mussolini was shot. When the fighting stopped, following the dropping of two atomic bombs on Japan, 50 million people had been killed. Defeated France and exhausted Britain gradually came to realize they were no longer the major world powers they had once been. In the decades following the war their empires slipped away from them.

Certain of victory, the 'Big Three', Churchill (right), Roosevelt (centre) and Stalin, meet in Yalta in February, 1945, to decide the fate of the post-war world.

42

The **Soviet Union** had fought the **Nazi** armies from Moscow back through eastern Europe and all the way to Berlin. Stalin had seen his country twice attacked by the **West** in twenty years, and he was determined this should not happen again. Soviet soldiers stayed in East Germany and eastern Europe, and the Soviets set up communist regimes in all the nations between themselves and West Germany. These so-called 'buffer states' were a barrier against further attack. Only when the Soviet Union collapsed in 1991 were the countries of eastern Europe allowed to choose their own governments.

Determined that there should be 'no more Pearl Harbors' the USA turned away from **isolationism**, and maintained a military presence in Europe and throughout the world. Today, France, Britain and Germany now strive for closer political ties within the European Union, and the thought of war between them is hard to imagine. Perhaps the most positive lesson learned from the war has been in the success of the United Nations especially compared to the failure of the League of Nations which preceded it.

The war in Europe comes to an end. A Russian soldier flies the Soviet flag from the Berlin Reichstag parliament on 30 April 1945.

The United Nations
The United Nations was set up in San Francisco in 1945. The principal of racial equality was written into its charter. Additionally, instead of relying only on economic **sanctions** to enforce its rulings, it was given military 'teeth' in the form of fighting forces from member states. Over the last half century, the UN has been involved in major conflicts throughout the world, from the Middle East and the Balkans to former **colonial** territories in Africa, where its troops are most often deployed in trouble spots in a peace-keeping role, keeping warring factions apart.

Timeline

1889	Birth of Adolf Hitler
1917	Lenin leads Bolshevik revolution in Russia
1918	March: Russia surrenders to Germany at the treaty of Brest-Litovsk
	November: World War One ends with Germany's armies in full retreat
1919	June: Treaty of Versailles
	September: Treaty of Germain-en-Laye with Austria
1920	Treaty of Trianon with Hungary
1921	Hitler becomes leader of the Nazi party
1922	Mussolini seizes power in Italy
1923	Nazi Beer Hall Putsch in Munich leads to arrest and imprisonment of Hitler
	Occupation of the Ruhr
1924	Dawes Plan restructures German reparations
1928	Stalin becomes leader of the Soviet Union
1929	Young Plan further reduces and restructures reparations
	September: Wall Street Crash leads to world-wide economic depression
1931	Japan invades Manchuria
1933	Hitler and Nazis come to power in Germany
1934	Hitler and Mussolini first meet
1935	Italy invades Abyssinia
1936	March: German troops move into the Rhineland
	July: Spanish Civil War begins (ends 1939)
	October/November: Germany, Italy and Japan declare themselves allied as 'Axis' powers
1937	Japan invades rest of China
1938	January: Nanjing falls to Japanese army and more than 100,000 are massacred
	March: Germany invades Austria and unites the two countries
	September: Munich agreement allows Germany to occupy Sudetenland in Czechoslovakia
1939	March: German army moves beyond the Sudetenland into Czechoslovakia
	August: Nazi-Soviet Pact
	September: Germany invades Poland
	Britain and France declare war on Germany
1941	June: Germany invades the Soviet Union
	December: Japan attacks Pearl Harbor and the USA joins World War Two
	Germany declares war on the USA
1943	Italy surrenders
1945	Germany and Japan defeated
	United Nations founded

Further reading

Reference Books

Causes and Consequences of the Second World War, Stewart Ross, Evans,1995

Days that shook the world – Pearl Harbor, Paul Dowswell, Hodder Wayland, 2002

Leading Lives – Adolf Hitler, David Taylor, Heinemann Library, 2002

Leading Lives – Benito Mussolini, David Downing, Heinemann Library, 2001

Leading Lives – Josef Stalin, David Downing, Heinemann Library, 2001

Questioning History: The Causes of World War II, Stewart Ross, Hodder Wayland 2002

Twentieth Century Leaders – Hitler, Paul Dowswell, Hodder Wayland, 2002

Novels and stories

I Can Never Go Home Again, Stewart Ross, Evans, 2002

The Machine Gunners, Robert Westall, Macmillan, 1994

The Silver Sword, Ian Serraillier, Puffin Books, 1993

War Boy, A Country Childhood, Michael Foreman, Puffin Books, 1991

For older readers

The Dark Valley – A Panorama of the 1930s, Piers Brendon, Pimlico, 2001

Hitler and Stalin – Parallel Lives, Alan Bullock, Fontana, 1993

The Origins of the Second World War, R.J. Overy, Longman, 1998

Websites

http://www.iwm.org.uk/

(Lots of fascinating material in the Imperial War Museum site.)

http://www.bbc.co.uk/history/war/wwtwo/hitler_1. shtml

(The BBC site is useful and gives a good account of many aspects of Hitler's life and his time as leader of Germany.)

Glossary

alliances agreements between countries that wish to support one another

allies broadly, meaning people, political parties or countries working together. Specifically, **Allies** refers to Britain and its empire, France and its empire and US forces in World Wars One and Two.

anarchist person who believes in the abolition of government

appeasement policy of keeping an enemy from doing more harm by giving in to some of their demands

armistice agreement to stop fighting

authoritarian demanding strict obedience to government

Axis alliance of Germany, Japan and Italy and other countries during World War Two

Bolshevik name given to the communists who seized power in Russia in 1917

civil war war fought between people of the same country

colonies countries owned and controlled by another country

communist believer in communism, a political system in which the state controls the wealth and industry of a country

concentration camp prison camp for civilian prisoners where they are often treated very brutally

conscription compulsory service in the armed forces

conservative preferring the preservation of established customs and traditions at the expense of new ideas

constitution political ideas which determine how a state is run

corruption in politics, a state of affairs where political decisions are decided by bribes and other favours, rather than any right or wrong considerations

cronies in politics, members of a party who owe their job in government to the fact that have a personal friendship with senior members of that party

cult of personality deliberate creation of a god-like image of a political leader, characteristic of states governed by a dictator.

delegates people representing an organization, region or country at a conference

democracy rule of a country by a government elected by the people

depression in economic terms, a period in time when businesses do badly and many people are unemployed and poor

dictatorship political situation where one person has absolute power to rule a country

diplomacy conduct of relations between countries

empire collection of colonies

fascism political philosophy opposed to communism and democracy, which glorifies power, military might and nationalism

ghetto part of a city where people of the same race or nationality live

illiterate unable to read or write

intelligentsia highly educated members of a society

isolationism in politics, the process of remaining free from alliances with other nations, or becoming involved with the affairs of other nations

left-wing in political terms this means leaning towards a socialist or communist viewpoint

liquidate destroy

motorized troops troops which travel by some form of motorized transport, as opposed to on foot

nationalist someone who wants his or her country to be independent of its colonial masters. This term can also refer to someone who unreasonably puts the interests of his or her country before all other countries.

natural resources naturally occurring materials such as coal or iron ore or foodstuffs to which a country has access

Nazi member of the National Socialist Party in Germany during Hitler's time. The philosophy of Nazism is basically the same as fascism.

neutral not being involved in conflict

propaganda misleading information that is used to try to persuade people to adopt a certain viewpoint

protectionism economic term broadly meaning buying goods made in your own territory and trying to prevent imports by imposing tariffs

purge in this case, a term relating to the widespread killing or imprisonment of sections of Soviet society perceived by Stalin to be a threat to his communist regime.

radical someone who supports extreme changes. A radical change is a big change.

raw material naturally occurring materials such as iron ore or rubber which can be turned into manufactured products by industry

reconciliation settling of quarrels and resentments between former enemies

republican someone who does not support a monarchy

revolution politically, a rebellion that leads to the overthrow of a government

right-wing in political terms, leaning towards a more conservative viewpoint. Fascists and Nazis are extreme right-wing political groups.

sanctions withholding of goods and raw materials exported to a country, to express disapproval of that country's actions

share financial term for a document showing an investment in a company, ownership of which entitles a person to some of that company's profits

socialist someone who supports the political system whereby a country's wealth is shared equally and where some of the main industries are run by the government

sphere of influence political term meaning an area of the world where one country feels it should be allowed to intervene

Soviet Union another name for the Union of Socialist Soviet Republics (USSR), a communist country including Russia

SS elite Nazi troops

stalemate situation in which neither side can win

stock market financial institution where shares are sold

strikes refusing to work as a way of making a protest

trade unions organized groups of workers set up to improve pay and working conditions

unemployment when people do not have jobs

West, Western political rather than geographical term for the rich industrialized countries of northern and western Europe, North America, Australia and New Zealand

Index